TELL ME WHY, TELL ME HOW

HOW DO WAVES FORM?

WIL MARA

 **Marshall Cavendish**
Benchmark
New York

Published by Marshall Cavendish Benchmark
An imprint of Marshall Cavendish Corporation

This publication represents the opinions and views of the author based on Wil Mara's personal experience, knowledge, and research. The information in this book serves as a general guide only. The author and publisher have used their best efforts in preparing this book and disclaim liability rising directly and indirectly from the use and application of this book.

Other Marshall Cavendish Offices:
Marshall Cavendish International (Asia) Private Limited, 1 New Industrial Road, Singapore 536196 • Marshall Cavendish International (Thailand) Co Ltd. 253 Asoke, 12th Flr, Sukhumvit 21 Road, Klongtoey Nua, Wattana, Bangkok 10110, Thailand • Marshall Cavendish (Malaysia) Sdn Bhd, Times Subang, Lot 46, Subang Hi-Tech Industrial Park, Batu Tiga, 40000 Shah Alam, Selangor Darul Ehsan, Malaysia

Marshall Cavendish is a trademark of Times Publishing Limited.

All websites were available and accurate when this book was sent to press.

Library of Congress Cataloging-in-Publication Data
Mara, Wil.
 How do waves form? / by Wil Mara.
 p. cm. — (Tell me why, tell me how)
 Summary: "Provides comprehensive information on the process of waves forming" —Provided by publisher.
 Includes index.
 ISBN 978-0-7614-4829-7
 1. Waves—Juvenile literature. 2. Wave—motion, Theory of—Juvenile literature. I. Title.
 QC157.M37 2011
 551.46'3—dc22
 2009041098

Photo research by Candlepants Incorporated

Cover Photo: Shutterstock

The photographs in this book are used by permission and through the courtesy of:
Shutterstock: 1, 10. *Getty Images*: Gary Brettnacher, 4; Sean Davey, 5, 12, 13; Richard du Toit, 6; Nacivet, 8; Mike Hill, 9; Angelo Cavalli, 11; Philip Long, 14; Biwa Inc, 15; Johner, 16; Vast Photography, 18; Macduff Everton, 19; John Lund, 20; Warren Bolster, 21; Jutta Klee, 24; Katarina Stefanovic, 17. *Alamy Images*: Martin Bond, 7. *Photo Researchers Inc.*: Gary Hincks, 22-23.

Editor: Joy Bean
Publisher: Michelle Bisson
Art Director: Anahid Hamparian
Series Designer: Alex Ferrari

Printed in Malaysia (T)

1 3 5 6 4 2

CONTENTS

It is fun just to watch waves roll onto the beach.

It Starts in the Sky

Have you ever stood on a beach and watched the ocean? The water rises up, then goes back down. Then up again, then down again. What you are seeing are **waves**. You may notice that some are gentle as they tumble forward until they disappear. Others, however, seem to crash hard onto the sand. Waves can occur in many different sizes and strengths. Most are harmless, but some can be very dangerous.

Some waves are so strong and large that people, such as surfers, use them for sport.

The typical wave you see on the beach usually comes from far out in the ocean. A wave does not really start in the water, but in the sky! Ocean waves begin with the wind. Because of this, they are often called **wind waves**. And since they are on the surface of the water, they are sometimes also called **surface waves**.

Wind waves, or surface waves, appear on the surface of the water and are very small.

Wind is a form of **energy**. That means it has power and force. Blow into the palm of your hand. You can feel the air, right? What you feel is energy going from your mouth to your hand. This is wind energy—and it can have a powerful effect on water.

These are surface waves as seen from a helicopter.

When wind blows down onto a body of water, it makes the water move around. Some of the energy from the wind also goes *into* the water. This is the start of a wave.

7

When the wind is blowing very lightly, water will ripple.

A Recipe for Waves

The size and strength of a wave depends on a few different things. Think of it like a recipe for food. The main ingredient in a wave is wind. And there are three important parts—the speed of the wind, how much water the wind is blowing on, and how long the wind blows.

Think of the speed of wind as the wind's strength. If the wind is blowing slowly, it may cause only a few **ripples** on the water. If the wind blows hard and fast, however, the waves will be much larger. This is because strong winds put more energy into the water.

Wind also has size—that is, a strong gust of wind can either blow over a small area of water or a very large area. The larger

If the wind is blowing heavily, rough waters will occur.

the area, the larger the waves will be. And the larger the waves are, the more power they will have.

The final ingredient in the wave recipe is time. The longer a gust of wind blows, the more energy it will put into the water. Imagine the candles on a birthday cake. If you blow on them very quickly, you might not put them all out. But if you blew for, say, ten seconds without stopping, they would all go out for sure!

The size and strength of a wave depends on how much wind there is. Just as with blowing out the candles on a cake, the longer you blow, the stronger the wind.

Now I Know!

What will a light wind that dies out quickly cause water to do?

Ripple.

Some of the most powerful winds come from storms. A hurricane, for example, has all the best ingredients to make big waves. It has winds that are very fast, blow over a large area of the water, and blow for a long time. That is why the ocean is a dangerous place to be during a hurricane.

A hurricane caused the powerful—and destructive—waves seen here.

While it looks like the water that makes up waves is constantly moving forward, the truth is that most of the water stays where it is and wind moves through the water instead.

On the Move

Once a wave starts in the ocean, it begins to move forward, toward the shore. An important thing to know is that a wave moves up and down, just like a squiggly line. However, the water itself does not move forward with the wave. So if a wave travels ten feet, the water does not also move ten feet forward. Wave energy simply moves *through* the water. The water will swirl around, but it mostly stays where it is.

A large amount of energy goes into a wave this big.

As this wave energy moves away from the spot where it began, it will create not just one wave but a group of them. This is called a **wave chain**. Again, think of the example of the squiggly line. The highest points in the squiggly line are the wave's **crests**. The lowest points are the wave's **troughs**.

A group of waves flow toward the beach.

The length of one wave can be figured out by measuring the distance from one crest to the next. In a small wave chain, the waves may be only a few feet apart. In a large and powerful chain, they may be hundreds of feet apart.

Sometimes waves crash into each other. When this happens, one of two things happens. The two waves either die out as a result of the collision, or they combine and make one new wave—a much stronger one!

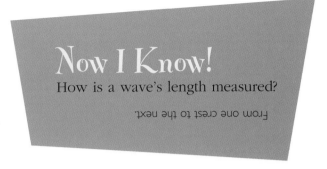

This laboratory photo shows the crest and trough of a wave.

15

Most waves that reach the shore roll softly onto the sand, causing no harm to anyone.

The Big Crash

Some waves reach dry land. This forces a wave's energy to come to a stop. And this is when some very interesting things begin to happen.

As a wave moves closer to a beach, the water gets more and more **shallow**. Think of it like a ramp—the land runs upward. As a wave moves into this area, it starts to fall apart. It can no longer move in its up-and-down motion, because the land underneath it gets in the way.

When a wave gets close to the shore, it loses energy and begins to crash onto itself.

The energy in the wave is now forced to pile up on itself. It is similar to blowing too much air into a balloon. When a balloon cannot hold any more air, the air has no place else to go, so the balloon bursts. Waves are like this when they reach

The energy in a wave is similar to that of air being blown into a balloon. The balloon can only hold so much air before it bursts. With a wave, when it has too much energy, it breaks apart.

the shore. When they have nowhere left to go, all their energy builds up for a moment. Then the wave breaks apart. There is no more water to hold the wave's energy.

Waves with enough energy in them will come crashing into the shore.

Small waves, called chops, will run into the beach on a day that has very little wind.

All Waves Big and Small

There are many different types of waves. The smallest are sometimes called ripples or **chops**. These do not get very large or last very long. A light gust of wind can create many ripples and chops that die out quickly. You may have heard someone say that the ocean is choppy. That means there is a lot of light wind causing little chops to appear all over the water.

Larger wind waves are called **swells**. These are the waves you see crashing onto the beach most often. Swells come in a wide variety of

When a wave gets very large, it begins to curl, such as the one seen here.

sizes. The smaller ones are fun to ride with a bellyboard or swim along with. The larger ones are good for surfing. They can grow to be ten or more feet and produce a **curl** at the crest, when the water up there begins to fall forward. Sometimes the curls hang down so far that a kind of water tunnel is created. These can be very dangerous to ride if you are not an experienced surfer.

Perhaps the most famous kind of wave is a **tsunami**. A tsunami is a huge and sudden rise in the water along a shoreline. When a tsunami hits, it is as if the entire ocean suddenly rolls forward! A tsunami can destroy houses and

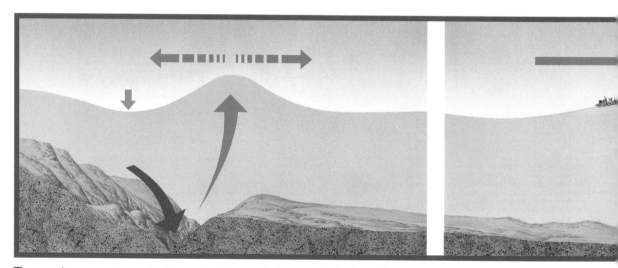

Tsunamis are not created by wind. Instead, the earth below the water shifts violently to create movement in the water.

other buildings, lift cars off the ground, knock down telephone poles, and harm many people.

A tsunami is not, however, created by wind. Instead, a tsunami is caused by sudden, violent activities under the water. The most common causes are volcanic eruptions, earthquakes, or landslides. All of these things can happen underwater. When they do, large masses of land move around. When the land underwater moves, that means the water over it also has to move. Think of it like sitting on a bench with your friends. If another friend comes along and wants to squeeze in, the rest of you have to move to make room.

When violent land movement takes place underwater, the sudden shift of water triggers a powerful wave of energy that begins moving through the water in every direction, like a circle that grows larger and larger. If the energy is still very

Most waves can be safely enjoyed in many different ways.

powerful when it reaches land, the water will swell outward before going back into the ocean.

Remember, though, that tsunamis are not like the

normal wind waves you see on an ocean or lake on any given day. Whether a wave is large enough for a surfer to ride or so small that it merely laps the wet sand, most of them begin in the sky with something as simple as an afternoon breeze.

# Activity

This is a fun, quick, and easy way to help you not only understand how wave energy moves through water, but also how the water itself moves only up and down.

WHAT YOU WILL NEED
- A bathtub (or a very large plastic tub)
- A toy that floats, such as a rubber duck or plastic boat

WHAT TO DO
1. Fill the tub about halfway with warm water.

2. Let the water become still so there is no wave movement at all.

3. Set the toy on the water.

4. Put your hand in the water, then move it up and down to create outward-moving waves.

5. Notice how the toy stays pretty much in the same place. It will move up and down, but the waves move under it and then keep going.

 Glossary

chop—Small wave on the surface of a body of water that does not last long.

crest—The top of a wave; a wave's highest point.

curl—The overhanging part of a wave's crest.

energy—Any form of power.

ripple—Small wave on the surface of a body of water that does not last long.

shallow—The opposite of deep; having relatively little depth.

surface wave—Another name for a wind wave, used because wind waves occur on the surface of the ocean.

swell—A large and powerful wind wave. Swells have a wide range of size and strength.

trough—The bottom of a wave; a wave's lowest point.

tsunami—A wave of tremendous strength that is caused by a violent undersea event, such as a volcanic eruption, earthquake, or landslide.

wave chain—A series of waves.

wave—An energy force that moves in a continuous up and down motion.

wind wave—Movement in water caused by wind.

 # Find Out More

BOOKS

Mason, Paul. *Ocean in Motion! Surfing and the Science of Waves*. Bel Air, CA: Fact Finders, 2009.

Peppas, Lynn. *Ocean, Tidal, and Wave Energy: Power from the Sea*. New York: Crabtree Publishing, 2008.

Stiefel, Chana. *Tsunamis*. New York: Children's Press, 2009.

Woodward, John. *Voyage: Ocean*. New York: DK Children's Books, 2009.

WEBSITES

Energy Kids

www.eia.doe.gov/kids/energyfacts/sources/renewable/ocean.html

A website all about energy from the ocean.

Geography for Kids

www.kidsgeo.com/geography-for-kids/0130-the-hydrosphere.php

A page devoted to all things related to Earth's oceans.

What Makes Waves?

http://kids-educational-activities.suite101.com/article.cfm/what_makes_waves

Good basic information on wave creation, with some information on tsunamis.

Index

Page numbers in **boldface** are illustrations.